JN077701

SEI｜徳田邸
────── 京都　生きる喜び

西沢立衛
徳田佳世

SEI｜Tokuda House
────── Kyoto　Joy of Life

Ryue Nishizawa
Kayo Tokuda

目次　Table of Contents

生きる喜び
徳田佳世

この本では、京都で西沢立衛さんが設計した建築と、世｜SEIと名付けた家での活動を紹介します。

現代美術のキュレーターとして瀬戸内の直島で働いていた頃、上司だった秋元雄史さんに建築家を探すように言われ、建築雑誌で見て印象に残ったのが西沢さんでした。《ウィークエンドハウス》(1998)の光の取り入れ方がとてもきれいだったのと、《鎌倉の住宅》(2001)の開口の絶妙なプロポーションを見て、電話をかけたのが事の始まりです。西沢さんとはこれまでの20年間で、実現しなかったものも含めて8つの仕事をしました。
企画を担当した最大の仕事、《豊島美術館》(アート：内藤礼、2010)は、7年もの歳月がかかりましたが、美術家の内藤礼さんと西沢さんと実現した運命的なプロジェクトでした。

豊島美術館が完成し、次なる仕事のため、なにも縁のなかった京都へ移住しました。京都では、町並みや日常の暮らしのかけがえのなさに初めて目を開かされました。また、様々な職人とその手の技術を学び、現代美術だけではなく伝統工芸や食に携わる友人たちと時間を共にしながら、自らの使命や生き方について深く考えてきました。思い返せば、これまで会ってきたアーティストとも、食事をしながら他愛もない話をしている時に、その作家の作品やコンセプトが理解できたと思える瞬間がありました。

そして2015年、偶然、築100年を超える町家に出会い、この土地ならではの暮らしや芸術や文化を、様々な人たちと一緒に考え、次世代へ伝えていくための環境をつくろうと思いました。私自身は、西沢さんが設計した建築の中に「住む」という経験はなく、一体どうなるんだろうかと思って依頼しました。西沢さんに要望したのは「外から見ると町並みに馴染んでいて、中に入ると宝物のように感じる家」でした。

Joy of Life
Kayo Tokuda

This book introduces my house in Kyoto, designed by Ryue Nishizawa and named 卋 | SEI (meaning world and generations), as well as the activities that have taken place there.

When I was working as a contemporary art curator on Naoshima in Setouchi, the museum director at that time, Yuji Akimoto, asked me to propose an architect for a new pavilion. Ryue Nishizawa's works stood out among the buildings that I found in architectural magazines. I was particularly taken by the way light entered into his Weekend House (1998), as well as the bold proportions of the openings of his House in Kamakura (2001). Our relationship began with a phone call to his office. Over the course of the last 20 years, I have worked with Mr. Nishizawa on eight projects, including two that have not come to fruition.
One of the most memorable projects I curated was the fateful collaboration with Rei Naito and Ryue Nishizawa at the Teshima Art Museum (Art: Rei Naito, 2010), which took seven years from start to finish.

After the opening of the Teshima Art Museum, I took a job in Kyoto, a city I had never lived in before. For the first time, I became aware of the precious streetscapes and daily life of Kyoto. I had many chances to think deeply about my own purpose and way of living while learning from artisans about their hand-made crafts, and spending time with creative friends involved in traditional art and cuisine, as well as contemporary art. Looking back, there were times when I would suddenly feel like I grasped an artwork or concept of an artist friend while casually chatting over a meal.

Then in 2015, I came across a more than century-old *machiya* townhouse and resolved to create a place where people from different backgrounds could gather to think about distinctive ways of life, art, and culture, and forge a way of passing them to future generations. I did not have any personal experience living inside a structure designed by Mr. Nishizawa, and I was excited to imagine how it would turn out when I asked him. My request to Mr. Nishizawa was that he create a house that blends into the townscape on the outside, and is a physical and spiritual treasure on the inside.

京都の町家のリノベーション
西沢立衛

初めて徳田さんとお会いしたのは2001年、直島での仕事を通してでした。その頃から、「いつか住宅を建てたい」という話をされていたことをこの京都で思い出しました。徳田さんから最初に「宝物がほしい」という言葉をもらって始まったプロジェクトでした。

これまでもリノベーションのプロジェクトをやったことはありましたが、《徳田邸》は木造ならではの魅力がありました。自分でゼロからつくっていくというよりは、古いものとの調和を考えることが課題でした。可能な限り既存のものは残しています。
建築をつくる際に、「先行する秩序」のうえで創造するということは間違いなくあると思います。ここでは、京都の町家の言語、既にそこにある形やディテールに気付かされました。京都で建築をつくることの難しさ、町家をリノベーションするという難しさの両方がありました。
既存の二棟の町家は、前面道路から向かって左側（南棟）がファサードがモルタルで覆われていて、右側（北棟）は割と伝統的な姿が残っていました。歪んでいた軸組をちゃんと水平・垂直にして現代的な構造計算をし、施工をする時の基準にもしています。南棟はファサードを新たにつくり、内部は骨組を見せて大きな気積を設け人が集うための空間に、北棟では通り庭を復活させ、上下をつなげる吹き抜けかつ風の通り道としています。
二棟の界壁の1階にも2階にも穴を穿ち、行き来できるようにすることで、互いに連携させて使うことも、独立させることもできます。徳田さんは、おそらく集会所やサロンそのものを求めていたのではなく、なにか特別な場所が必要だったのだと思います。ここが住宅であちらが集会所というように使い方を限定しない方が良いと考えました。お施主さんから出される設計条件というのは、ユーザーや住まい手としての問題意識が表れているものですが、それらに直接的に答えるのではなく、その問題の起源を探っていくことで、別の提案によって解決できる可能性があります。

住宅の設計というのは、どういうキッチンにするか、書斎にどう机を配置するか、どんなソファやカーテンにするか……、といった小さなことから、人間の生き方といったとても大きなことまで、際限なく考えることができるおもしろさがあります。
僕がこれまで感動を覚えた住宅は、住まい方や生き方が想像されるものです。住宅は、建てるだけでは未完成で、人間が住むことによって住宅になっていくのです。

左：模型での検討。　右：施工中。南棟2階の床を撤去して吹抜けの空間に。
Left: Planning model　Right: Under construction. The upper floor of the south wing was removed to create a high-ceilinged space.

Renovation of a Kyoto Machiya
Ryue Nishizawa

I first met Kayo Tokuda in 2001 when she was hard at work on her first pavilion project as a curator on Naoshima. When she came to me about the Kyoto machiya, I remembered that she had mentioned early in our relationship that she wanted to build a house someday, and that she wanted me to design it when the time came. The project began with her remark that she wanted "a spiritual treasure," a place where joy in life could be found in beauty.

I have done renovation projects in the past, but the Tokuda House had a particular charm as a wooden structure. The challenge was to figure out how to harmonize with the old building, rather than simply create something from scratch. I preserved original elements as much as possible.
When building a structure, there are certainly cases when it is necessary to create something on top of a pre-existing order. In this project, I became familiar with the existing shapes and details that form the vernacular of Kyoto machiya architecture. Both construction in Kyoto and renovation of a machiya building presented particular difficulties.
Of the two wings of the machiya building, the left side when seen from the front street (south wing) had a façade covered in mortar, while the right side (north wing) remained relatively traditional in appearance. We straightened out the deformed skeleton and performed modern structural analysis in order to establish a basis for construction measurements. The south wing received a new facade. Inside, the skeleton was exposed and the space was turned into a large volume to allow for gatherings of people. We restored the north wing's *tōri-niwa* (passageway between the entrance and back garden), which serves as a vertical space to connect the upper and lower floors of the building and allow for air circulation.
Openings were created in the first- and second-floor walls separating the two wings in order to make it possible to move back and forth and use the spaces together or independently. I got the sense that Ms. Tokuda wanted a special kind of space, rather than simply a gathering place or salon. It seemed appropriate to avoid a clear separation in function between the house and the gathering area. The awareness of the user or resident is reflected in the design conditions they request. Seeking out the source of that awareness makes it possible to address issues through alternative proposals rather than directly.

The interesting part of designing a house is the opportunity to think endlessly about things both small and large, from the shape of the kitchen, the placement of the desk in the study, or the type of sofa or curtains, to pondering the human way of life.
I have been most affected by houses that conjure a certain way of inhabiting and living. A house remains unfinished after construction; it becomes a house when people live in it.

南棟。正面の平格子は新設。右上の虫籠窓にはアクリルが嵌められている。
The south wing. The *hira-gōshi* lattice on the front façade is new. The narrow *mushiko-mado* windows in the upper right corner are fitted with acrylic.

ものづくりの緊張

鳥居厚志

《徳田邸》の工事では、徳田さんと西沢さんの様々なやり取りや、西沢さんの設計プロセスを肌で感じることができて、自分たちにとって大きな財産になりました。普段、伝統的な数寄屋建築も手掛けているなかで、既にある型に従ってつくっていくことも多いのですが、ここでは、西沢さんの好みがあり、徳田さんの個性があり、予算や工期などの制限もあり、正解がわからないなかで試行錯誤していく緊張感がありました。工事の途中で西沢さんが「これはディテールが勝負だ」と言っているのを聞き、大変なプレッシャーになりました。構造補強では、新設基礎と柱の接合金物等が意匠に影響しないよう、桃李舎の枡田さんと検討を重ね、見えない部分の納まりにも気を配りました。設計と施工が同時に進んでいくなかで、柔軟に対応していただけるベテランの大工さんに頼めたことは、とても大きかったです。また、京都の土壁は、種類が豊富なのですが、色味や風合いを共有することは予想以上に難しく、サンプルを何度もつくり直しながら西沢さんたちと共に検討していきました。南棟の床暖房入りの土間コンクリートは、目地を入れずになるべくクラックが発生しないようにするという難しい課題がありました。打設時期が年末の寒い時期だったのですが、緻密なコンクリートを夜中までかけて左官屋さんに仕上げてもらいました。徳田さんには、床暖房の使用を1年目はできるだけ控えていただくようにお願いしたのですが、実際は2年間も控えてくださっていたようです。

この建築がなにを目指していたのかがわかったのは、完成後でした。つくり手とすまい手の信頼関係がなければ成り立たない、徳田さんの生き方や願いが表現された建物だと思います。建築の素晴らしさ、住むことの楽しさはもちろんですが、作品の中に住み続ける難しさもあると思います。私もこの仕事を通して、ひとつひとつの課題に安易に答えを出してはいけないと考えるようになりました。

左: 柱と基礎は、新たな金物のジョイントでピン接合としている。壁を修繕するための竹小舞掻き。
右: 土間コンクリート打設。柱の足元は、保護とコンクリートとの取り合いのため、銅板が巻かれている。
Left: The columns are secured to the foundation using pins in new metal joints. Scouring the bamboo lattice as part of repairing a wall.
Right: Pouring the concrete floor. Copper plates are wrapped around the feet of the columns to protect them and improve their compatibility with concrete.

左: 土壁のサンプルをつくるための調整。 右: 土壁塗り。
Left: Adjusting consistency for earthen wall samples. Right: Spreading an earthen wall.

7種類の壁仕上げのサンプル。力強さと美しさが求められた。
Samples of seven different types of wall finishes.
Strength and beauty are demanded.

The Strains of Creation
Atsushi Torii

I learned a great deal during the construction of the Tokuda House from observing up close the exchanges between Ms. Tokuda and Mr. Nishizawa, as well as Mr. Nishizawa's creative process. My experience working on traditional *sukiya-zukuri* architecture has accustomed me to making things fit within pre-existing forms. However, in this project, I was strained to a certain degree as I groped for the right answer while trying to accommodate Nishizawa-san's preferences, Tokuda-san's individuality, and budgetary and schedule constraints.

I felt intense pressure when I heard Mr. Nishizawa say during the construction that "the details will make or break this project." I consulted closely with Ms. Yoko Masuda of Tōri-sha to painstakingly design earthquake resistance measures in such a way that the metal fittings that secure the columns to the new foundation would not detract from the design, and worked until we were satisfied even with the hidden parts. With design and construction proceeding simultaneously, it made all the difference that I could call on a veteran carpenter who was able to adapt. Kyoto is known for having a wide range of earthen walls, but it was more difficult than we had imagined to match coloring and texture, so we created numerous samples in discussion with Mr. Nishizawa. The south wing features a jointless concrete floor with in-floor heating, which was particularly challenging to finish without cracks. Construction took place during the cold winter months, but the craftsman stayed until midnight in order to finish precisely setting the concrete. I asked Ms. Tokuda to avoid using the floor heating during the first year as much as possible, and she actually held out for two years.

It was not until the house was complete that I got a sense of what this house was meant to be. The building feels like an expression of Ms. Tokuda's way of life and her euphoria. This could not have been achieved without trust between the resident and the people involved in creating it. Aside from the elegance of the building and the joy of living there, I think that inhabiting a work of architecture comes with challenges. This project taught me that we must think carefully about how to solve every issue.

人間が思考した痕跡としてのディテール
西沢立衛

《徳田邸》は、全体の構成やストラクチャー、物の組み立ての秩序など、建築をつくる楽しさがありました。設計と施工が同時進行していく状況で、現場は大変でした。事務所でも色々なことを考えますが、やはり現場で考えたことも大きかったです。ただ僕は、現場の雰囲気に飲み込まれないよう、帰りの新幹線の中などで一旦距離をおいて冷静に考えることも大切にしています。
現場監督の鳥居さんとは、同じく京都で《森の屋根ときのこ》(協働: nendo、2013)という仕事で初めてご一緒しました。難しい形だったにもかかわらず、とても楽しそうに美しくつくってくださって、感銘を受けました。ここでまた一緒に仕事ができてうれしかったです。

《徳田邸》の仕事では、ディテールの重要さを改めて感じました。現代の建築は、引違いサッシからお風呂の給湯器に至るまで、各メーカーがつくった既成の部品を寄せ集めて建築をつくるので、開口部やドア、柱や壁といった部分を見ると、ほとんど個性はありません。ルネサンスの建築家ブルネレスキは、設計と施工の両方をやっていましたが、建設だけでなく石材などのパーツの発注まで自身で行っていたそうで、細部から全体まで、独創的なものになっています。ミースやル・コルビュジエ、ライトといった初期モダニズムの建築家の作品も、写真でバックマリオンの部分を見ただけで誰がつくったものかがわかります。ディテールという言葉は難しい言葉ですが、簡単に言えば工夫のことです。人間が考えて、工夫してものを組み立てる、そのことです。工夫のない建築は、ディテールのない建築で、見ていてあまりおもしろくありません。
町家というのは、色々な人が考えてきたディテールの宝庫で、大変勉強になりました。京都には町並みがあり、個々の建築のディテールには奥行きがあって見飽きない。人間が思考し工夫してきた痕跡があるのです。

Details as Traces of Human Thought
Ryue Nishizawa

The true pleasure of creating the Tokuda House was considering the building's overall organization and structure, and the order within which elements come together.

It was a challenging project because the design and construction were progressing simultaneously. I come up with many ideas in my office, but I also gained valuable insights on-site. Still, I am a believer in the importance of getting some distance, such as on the train ride home, and thinking with a cool head so as not to lose perspective.

I first met Mr. Torii, the construction supervisor, when we worked together on an exhibition installation with Ms. Tokuda in Kyoto called Roof & Mushrooms (a collaboration with nendo, 2013). I was impressed by how beautifully Mr. Torii finished that structure, despite its challenging shape. I was pleased to be able to work with him again on this project.

Throughout the Tokuda House project, I was reminded of the importance of details. Contemporary buildings are constructed by assembling a wide range of manufactured components, from sliding window sashes to water heaters, which means that parts such as openings and doors, or columns and walls, have few distinctive features. The Renaissance architect Filippo Brunelleschi did both design and construction, and his buildings reflect his creativity from the smallest details to the entire structure because he was particular about ordering his own stone and other components. The works of early modernist architects such as Mies van der Rohe, Le Corbusier, and Frank Lloyd Wright can also be identified simply by looking at elements such as the back mullions in photographs. "Detail" is a tricky term, but it essentially means cleverness. Details arise when humans use their minds to come up with a clever way to assemble things. A building that has not been cleverly conceived is a building without details, blandly uninteresting to the eye.

I learned a great deal from working on a *machiya*, which is a cornucopia of details cleverly crafted by many artisans. I never tire of admiring the streetscapes of Kyoto and the substantial details of each building—all traces of human thought and cleverness.

敷地面積　93㎡
建築面積　63.5㎡
延床面積　88.2㎡
　　1階63.5㎡　2階24.7㎡
建蔽率　68%（許容80%）
容積率　95%（許容300%）

用途地域　近隣商業地域
その他の地域地区　準防火地域
前面道路幅員　東5.6m

設計期間　2015年4月-12月
施工期間　2015年5月-2016年4月

設計
建築・監理 | 西沢立衛建築設計事務所
　　　　　　西沢立衛 松井元靖 東出優子
構造 | 桃李舎 枡田洋子 田村沙咲

施工管理
アトリエ九間　鳥居厚志

仮設工事 | 西山仮設　西山憲治
解体・基礎・石工事 | 北村建設　北村久人
木工事 | 中善広岡工務店　広岡直樹 吉良利生
瓦工事 | 西明瓦店　西明男
板金・軒工事 | 水内板金工作所　水内雅輝
左官工事 | 中須左官店　中須仁隆 薬師剛

竹小舞 | 森川佳竹材店　森川佳明
木製建具工事 | 長野建具店　長野孝司
ガラス工事 | 奥村ガラス店　奥村寿幸
塗装工事 | 犬亥塗装　乾賢一
畳工事 | 高室畳工業所　高室節生
美装工事 | 中野洗工店　藤田博
キッチン・箱階段・机・椅子 | 樹輪舎　八十原誠
手洗桶 | 中川木工芸比良工房　中川周士
構造金物 | 牧本金属　牧本晴男
ステンレス加工 | 北川晃
電気設備工事 | 稲葉電設　稲葉彰久
空調設備工事 | 吉村住設　吉村務
給排水・ガス設備工事 | 三洋工業　藤田古京
庭園工事 | 石川庭園　石川佳

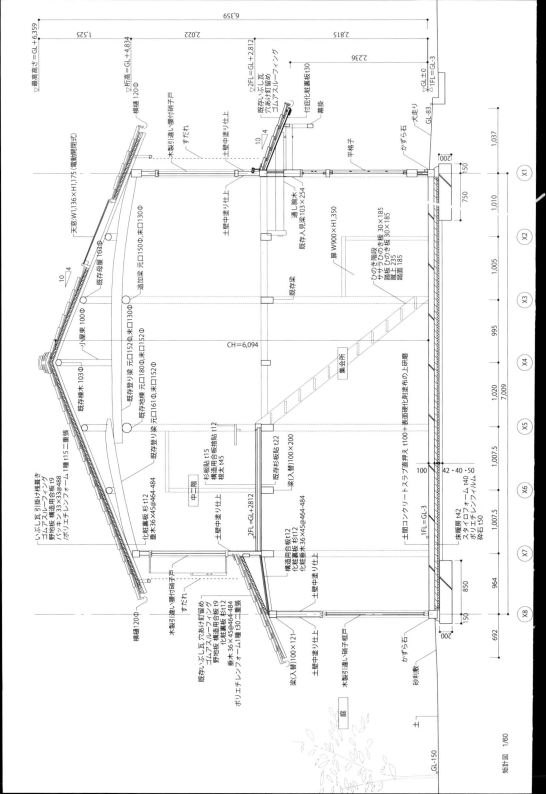

矩計図 1/60

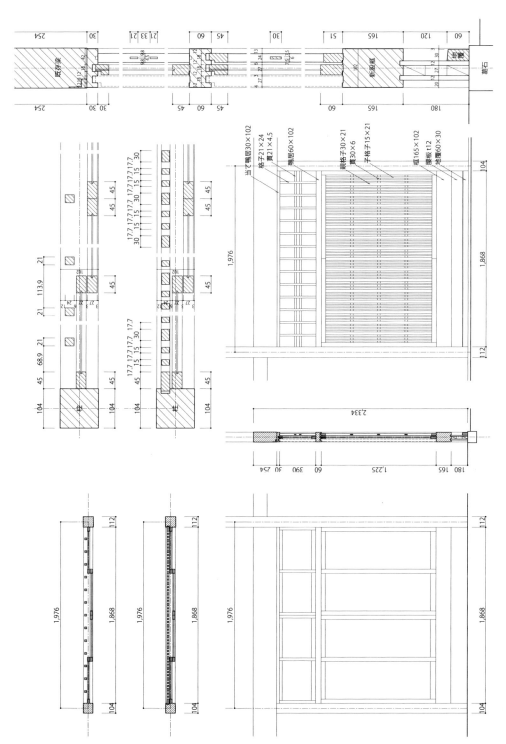

平格子詳細図

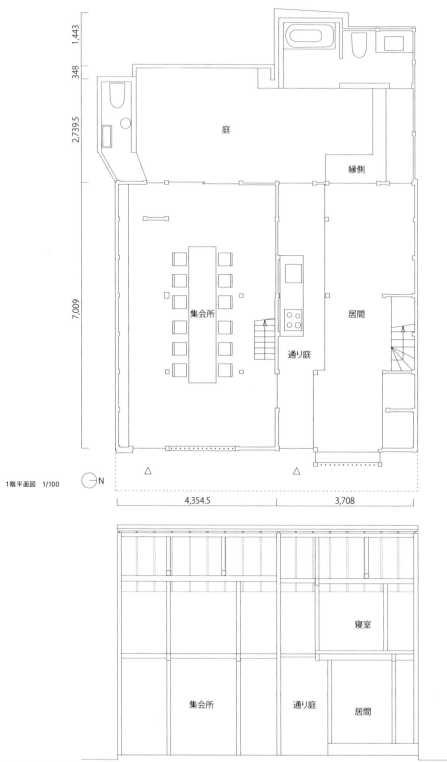

1,443

348

2,739.5

7,009

庭

縁側

集会所

通り庭

居間

1階平面図　1/100

N

4,354.5

3,708

寝室

集会所

通り庭

居間

南北方向断面図　1/100

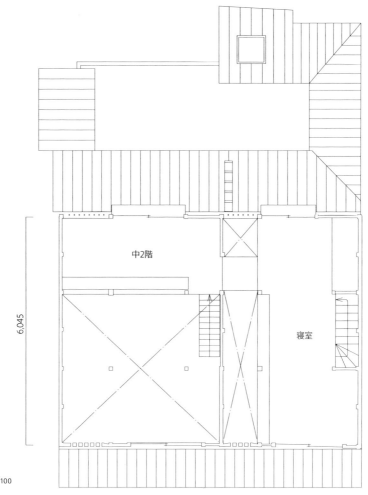

中2階

6,045

寝室

2階平面図　1/100

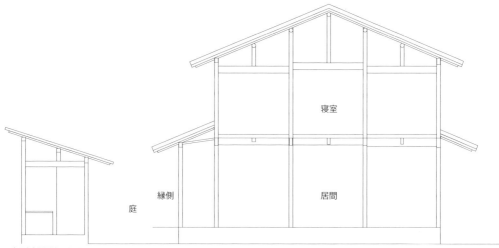

寝室

縁側

庭

居間

東西方向断面図　1/100

家との共感
徳田佳世

家が完成して最初の半年間、毎朝そこで起きる度に、事の重大さを感じさせられていました。長年、西沢さんの仕事を見てきたつもりですが、なにもわかっていなかったかのようです。人間の創造性、職人技の結晶であり、贈り物に敬意を覚えます。キュレーターとしては、プロジェクトが完成して公開されたり、写真に撮られて雑誌などで紹介されることに達成感を感じてきましたが、この家はそういうものではなかったのです。
今も、どんな教科書にも書かれていない方法で、生き方や建築と環境による精神への作用を学んでいるような気がします。西沢さんはいつも私に重要な言葉や考えを残していきます。たとえば、豊島美術館の周りの植栽をどうするか聞いた時、「なにもしない方がいい、その土地の自然な植生に任せればいい」と言っていたことを思い出します。環境と建築の関係を深く意識されてのことだったと後で気付かされました。

家ができて、ここに住みながら、より良い世界を築き残していくことを願って、いくつかの活動を始めています。私にとっては、家をつくり、そこで暮らし、生きていくということは、常設のサイトスペシフィック・プロジェクトと同じなのです。

Empathy for the House
Kayo Tokuda

For the first half year after the house was completed, I would wake up every morning with a sense of the significance of what had transpired. I had admired Mr. Nishizawa's architecture for many years, but it seems that I hadn't really understood it. I feel a deep sense of respect toward the gift of this house, a true crystallization of nature, human creativity and craftsmanship. As a curator, I feel a sense of accomplishment upon completing a project and opening it to the public, or seeing it photographed and introduced in magazines, but that was not the case with this house.
I continue to feel as if I am getting a unique education in architecture and how our environment influences the mind through physical experience. Mr. Nishizawa always leaves behind important words and ideas for me. For example, when I asked what to do about the landscaping around the Teshima Art Museum, he told me, "we won't do anything, just leave the island's vegetation to do its work." I realized later that he was deeply conscious of the relationship between the environment and architecture.

Since the house was completed and I took up residence here, I have started a number of activities in hopes of leaving my surroundings richer than I found them. For me, building a house, inhabiting and living within it, is a way of site-specific art project.

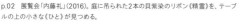

p.02　展覧会「内藤礼」(2016)。庭に吊られた2本の貝紫染のリボン《精霊》を、テーブルの上の小さな《ひと》が見つめる。

pp.06−07　南棟。白木の梁を新たに加え、一部傷んでいた柱を交換することで、構造が担保されている。土壁や漆喰は損傷の激しい部分のみ塗り直された。

pp.08−09　北棟。道路側の出格子窓は既存のもの。かつてあった通り庭を復活させている。箱階段は新設。

p.12　南棟の床。土間コンクリートの上に硬化剤を塗布し、研磨仕上げ。

p.13　新たにつくられたヒノキの階段と既存の壁。

p.14　通り庭とキッチン。界壁は、経年によってできた自然な凹凸を活かした仕上げ。

p.15　庭と縁側。水回り部分は新設。壁は60×90mmのヒノキ材が並べられている。縁側の材もヒノキ。

p.18左　北棟2階。

p.18右　屋号「卅」の暖簾がかけられた南棟の入口。

p.24　家具が入る前の集会所。

p.26　使われる器はすべて特注。伊賀の岸野寛による白と織部の緑の蕎麦猪口、5寸皿、7寸皿、高台の大皿など。グラスは京都の佐藤聡によるもので、米を研いだ際の水をイメージした半透明のものと、手に馴染む透明なものの2種。テーブルと椅子は西沢立衛によるデザインで、樹林舎の八十原誠が制作した。

p.27左　浴室。壁と床はモザイクタイル仕上げ、天井はヒノキ。

p.27右　居間と水回りをつなぐ廊下。ヒノキ材の隙間から光が入る。

p.02 Rei Naito Exhibition (2016). *The spirit* of two Tyrian purple-dyed ribbons hanging in the garden is gazed upon by a small *human* on the table.

pp.06-07 South wing. The structure was reinforced by the addition of new unvarnished beams and replacement of some damaged columns. Only the most damaged sections of the earthen walls and plaster were redone.

pp.08-09 North wing. The *degōshi-mado* (projecting lattice window) facing the street is original. The *tōri-niwa* passageway was restored. The *hako-kaidan* (staircase with storage) is new.

p.12 Floor of the south wing. The surface of the concrete was treated with a hardener before being polished.

p.13 Newly built cypress staircase and existing walls.

p.14 Tōri-niwa and kitchen. The separating wall was finished in a manner that accentuates the natural unevenness of age.

p.15 Garden and veranda. The bathing area is housed in a new structure. 60 x 90 mm cypress panels are used on the walls. Cypress wood is also used on the veranda.

p.18 Left: Second floor of the north wing.

p.18 Right: Entrance to the south wing with a curtain featuring the name of the space, 卅 | SEI.

p.24 The gathering space before furniture was installed.

p.26 All ceramics are custom made. The white and green Oribe-rim soba cups, 15-centimeter plates, 21-centimeter plates, and raised serving platters are made by Kan Kishino of Iga. The glasses are made by Satoshi Sato of Kyoto. There are two kinds of glasses: a semi-transparent type that evokes the look of water used to polish rice, and a transparent type that fits snugly in the hand. The table and chairs are designed by Ryue Nishizawa and fabricated by Makoto Yasohara of Jurinsha.

p.27 Left: Bathroom. The walls and floor are finished with mosaic tiles; the ceiling is cypress.

p.27 Right: Corridor between the living room and the bathing area. Light enters through gaps between the cypress boards.

あしたの畑

すべては希望となるため。

"畑"から始まる、食、器、祈りの場、住まい、交流の場をつくり、美しい景色を生み出すことを目指す。それは、人の暮らし方、知恵と技術がもたらす現代の美意識と哲学、そして次世代により良い社会を継承したいという願いを意識させる芸術活動である。また、日本の風土が持つ豊かさを、アーティストや建築家、料理人、職人たちが共に思考し、語り合い、共作、共存する機会でもある。

人間の欲により環境破壊が進み、思考の違いにより争いが絶えない世界、絶望と危機感を感じる人々の意識に、芸術を通して希望に満ちた社会を築くために、今をどう生き、各々がどのような役割を担い、行動に移すことで平和を目指すのかを問いかける。アートと農作を含めた暮らし、この小さなきっかけに関わる人ひとりひとりの意識と実践が、日本のある地域から始まり、世界中に広がればと願う。

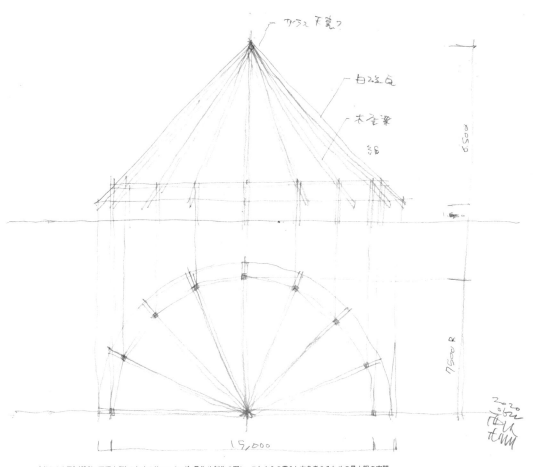

《考える小屋》（設計：西沢立衛）のためのドローイング。農作や制作の間に、これからの暮らし方を考えるための最小限の空間。
Drawing of A Thinker's Cabin designed by Ryue Nishizawa. A proposal for future housing as minimum space but maximum quality in minds and for experience.

TOMORROW FIELD

Creative act is hope.

TOMORROW FIELD endeavors to create a landscape that revolves around food, community, housing, communication, artifacts, and prayer. Our project originates on farmland in Kyoto.
TOMORROW FIELD is an art project whose aim is to deliver a rewarding life to future generations by bringing beauty, philosophy, and the lessons, skills, and knowledge of the past to a younger peer group. It is also about experiencing and sharing time and space with artists, architects, artisans, and chefs, and rediscovering the spiritual and natural gifts provided by the land and how to integrate this into modern life.

TOMORROW FIELD is project that questions the role of the arts in the future and one that yearns for the arts to be a generating force of peace among world citizens.

TOMORROW FIELD is a practice that starts with touching the soil as a way of saying a prayer. We hope that our small attempt to create a model for a society immersed in art and agriculture will spread from our small field in Japan throughout the world.

中川周士「あしたの畑—農業桶」2020、朽木の杉、銅、47cm×37cm
"Farm Bucket for Tomorrow" by Shuji Nakagawa, 2020, Kutsuki's cedar and bronze, 47cm×37cm

佐藤聡
「あしたの畑―水をうける器」2020
"Water Bowl for Tomorrow"
by Satoshi Sato, 2020

新里明士
「あしたの畑―木の記憶」2020
"Wooden Memory for Tomorrow"
by Akio Niisato, 2020

嘉戸浩、中川周士
「あしたの畑―唐紙の木っ端」2020
"*Karakami* Wooden Block for Tomorrow"
by Koh Kado and Shuji Nakagawa, 2020

SEI-kitchen

集い、美味しい食事をともにすることが人を幸せにする──楽しみながら、
真剣に食と環境に向き合っている料理人とアート・建築・環境、各分野の専門家を各回お招きし、
学び、語るひとときを共有する──この願いをかたちにする。

SEI-kitchen is to rethink harmonious relationship between nature and human through
discussions on food, art and architecture.

——第1回 2019.11.4
「FUTURE ART—食と建築」
献立：焼き栗
シェフ：藤田怜美（菓子職人）
ゲスト：西沢立衛（建築家）
お菓子について：昔食べた焼栗の香りと風景を表現。
京都に生息する栗の葉の中に栗の実が一粒。炙った栗羊羹の中には栗ムースとクリームブリュレが入り、伝統と現代がひとつになった季節のお菓子。

SEI-kitchen #1
"Future Art: Food and Architecture"
Menu: Seasonal sweets, YAKIGURI
Chef: Satomi Fujita, kashiya
Guest: Ryue Nishizawa, Architect
Ingredients: Chestnut cream brûlée and mousse inside steamed chestnut paste jelly. It looks like traditional Japanese candy outside but very modern inside.

——第2回 2019.11.10
「現代アートの思考法・前編：
アーティストはどんなふうに考えるのか？」
献立：おでん—アジア
シェフ：吉岡哲生（料理人）
ゲスト：秋元雄史（アートディレクター）
おでん｜出汁：牛すねとアンチョビ　具材：ちくわぶ、パパイヤ、大根、黄ニラ水餃子、パクチーさつま揚げ、ギンナン、しいたけ、ビーフン、セロリ、大谷渡り、赤かぶ、牛すね肉

SEI-kitchen #2
"How Does an Artist Think
When Creating A Work of Art?"
Menu: Oden-Asia
Chef: Tetsuo Yoshioka, Berangkat
Guest: Yuji Akimoto, Art Director
Ingredients: Chikuwabu flour paste, Papaya, Daikon radish, Yellow leek dumpling, Coriander in fried fish paste, Ginkgo, Shiitake mushroom, Celery, Asplenium antiquum, Rice noodles, Red turnip, Beef shank, Dashi soup: Beef shank and anchovies.

——第3回 2019.12.9
「現代アートの思考法・後編：ウォルター・デ・マリア」
献立：おでん—イタリア
シェフ：坂本健（料理人）
ゲスト：秋元雄史
おでん｜出汁：牛テール、鶏の手羽先、昆布、塩　具材：聖護院大根、小かぶ、原木椎茸、金時人参、平茸、海老芋、穴ごぼう、チーマディラーパ、九条ネギ、ロールキャベツ（牛テール大根もち）
卵とすっぽんのリゾット　米麹と生ハムの味噌　トッピング｜高菜のマスタード

SEI-kitchen #3
"Walter De Maria"
Menu: Oden-Italian
Chef: Ken Sakamoto, cenci
Guest: Yuji Akimoto
Ingredients: Shogoin kyoto daikon radish, Small turnip, Log shiitake mushroom, Kintoki carrot, Oyster mushroom, Shrimp-shaped taro root, Burdock with hole, Rape flower leaf, Kujo green onion, Stuffed cabbage with cow tail as radish rice cake. Dashi soup: Cow tai, Chicken wings, Konbu kelp, Salt. Risotto with semi-raw egg and suppon soft-shelled turtle soup. Miso with Kōji malted rice and prosciutto Topping: Takana leaf mustard

——第4回 2019.12.23
「アートを日本から見る・日本の外から見る」
献立：おぜんざい
シェフ：桑村祐子
ゲスト：神谷幸江（キュレーター）、林寿美（キュレーター）
おぜんざい：大根、出汁、小豆、とち餅、玄米餅、ごぼう、山椒

SEI-kitchen #4
"Seeing Art From Inside and Outside Japan"
Menu: Zenzai- soup with mochi
Chef: Yuko Kuwamura
Guest: Yukie Kamiya, Sumi Hayashi (curator)
Ingredients: Sweetened red beans, Genmai rice cake, Horse chestnut mochi, Dashi soup stock soup, Burdock, Sansho pepper

—— 第5回 2020.6.1「あしたの畑―味噌スープランチ」
献立：味噌スープ
シェフ：坂本健
あけぼの大豆を使った白味噌と米味噌　出汁：昆布、焙乾茶葉、もち麦　具：新たまねぎ、アスパラガス、クレソン、実山椒ピクルス

SEI-kitchen #5
"Miso Soup for Tomorrow"
Menu: Miso Soup
Chef: Ken Sakamoto
Miso: White miso and rice miso using Akebono soybeans
Dashi soup: Konbu kelp, Roasted tea leaves, Pearl barley tea
Ingredients: Season-fresh onion, Asparagus, Watercress, Green Japanese peppercorn pickles

—— 第6回 2020.7.19
「あしたの畑―オーガニック・ソウルフード」
献立：トマトスープカレー、大原の野菜―ヨーグルトと発酵野菜のソース
シェフ：坂本健、横山耕介、渥美彰人
カレー｜具：ジャガイモ、タマネギ、トマト、ナス、パプリカ、万願寺唐辛子、モロッコインゲン、ゆで卵　出汁：卵鶏、タマネギ、トマト、ニンジン、昆布、特製スパイスミックス（カイエンペッパー、カルダモン、クミン、黒胡椒、コリアンダーシード、フェンネルシード、レモングラス）酵素玄米ご飯：丸麦、黒米、玄米
サラダ｜大原の野菜：きゅうり、赤キャベツ、赤タマネギ、枝豆、ブルーベリー、まくわうり、ミディートマト、cenci 特製揚げ米　ドレッシング：大原産しば漬、新しょうがの赤紫蘇と梅酢漬け、大根ぬか漬け、水切りヨーグルトとホエイ、ハチミツ、レモン果汁、オリーブオイル、カルダモン
飲み物｜赤紫蘇のコンブチャ

SEI-kitchen #6
"TOMORROW FIELD—Organic Alimentation for Tomorrow"
Menu: Tomato soup curry, Local vegetables-Yogurt and fermented vegetable sauce
Chef: Ken Sakamoto, Kosuke Yokoyama, Akihito Atsumi (cenci)
Curry | Ingredients: Boiled egg, Eggplant, Manganji togarashi, Onion, Potato, Romano beans, Tomato (from Kyoto)
Soup: Carrot, Chicken, Kelp, Onion, Tomato, Spices (black pepper, cardamom, cayenne pepper, coriander seed, cumin, fennel seed, lemongrass)
Steamed and fried black rice: Black rice, Brown rice, Wheat berry
Salad | Local vegetables: Blueberry, Boiled green soybeans, Cenci special fried rice, Cucumber, Medium tomato, Oriental melon, Red cabbage, Red onion
Dressing: Japanese pickles with red shiso leaves, Red pickled ginger, Japanese pickled radish, Strained yogurt and whey, Honey, Lemon juice, Olive oil, Cardamom
Drink | Red shiso leaves Kombucha

墓地構想

Graveyard Concept

芸術の根源となる動機について思考を重ね、行き着いた結論が「祈り」、そして墓地がもつ意味だった。世界各国の墓地を訪れ、埋葬の方法や副葬品、壁画やオブジェ、建築といった芸術から、冥界での幸福を祈る空間として具現化された各時代の祈りのかたちに思いを馳せた。

死と向き合うことでどう生きるかを考え、心を動かす場所としての墓地を西沢立衛さんと構想し始めたのは、実は豊島美術館建設の最中だった。

以来10年以上にわたり、残された人々が生きる希望を取り戻す場所として、実現を望んでいる構想である。

Long contemplation of the motivations behind art led me to the concept of "prayer," and to the significance of the graveyard.

It has become customary for me to visit to graveyards and historical tombs when I journey around the world. In many locales, I have encountered burial methods, burial items, murals, architecture and artistic objects including sculpture, which evoke the sentiment of each era embodied in spaces of prayer for happiness in the afterlife.

I began thinking with Mr. Nishizawa about a graveyard, where visitors would face death and be moved to think about how to live, during the construction of the Teshima Art Museum.

This graveyard is conceived as a place of revitalization for people who are left behind, where artistic experience inspires hope for living in a setting in harmony with nature.

新里明士によってつくられた骨壷。
An urn by Akio Niisato.

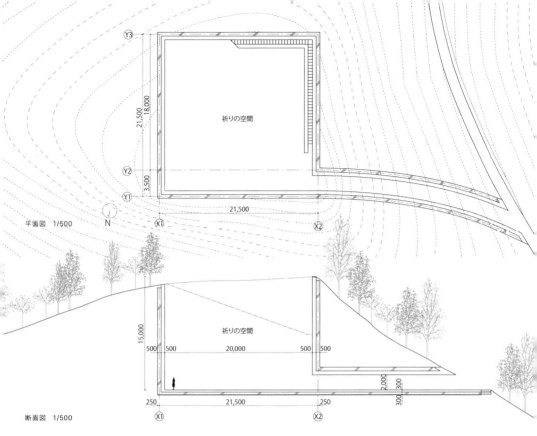

平面図 1/500 N

祈りの空間

21,500
18,000
3,500
21,500

Y3 Y2 Y1 X1 X2

断面図 1/500

祈りの空間

15,000
500 500 20,000 500 500
2,000
300 300

250 21,500 250

X1 X2

瀬戸内海に浮かぶ小さな無人島とその対岸の浜辺に計画された墓地構想である。浜辺には、数人が泊まれる小さな宿、無人島には、船着き場、散策路、墓標、休憩所、祈りの場がある。対岸の浜辺から島に小舟でアプローチし、散策路をめぐり、島にある木々や小川といった自然を感じながら、墓標、祈りの場を訪れ、島全体の環境を体験するというものだ。お墓は、森の中に、地形にしたがって、木々の合間に建てられる。人間が家を建てるのと同じように、谷や斜面、頂上、木の下など周辺環境に合わせて建つ。

祈りの場は、島の頂上から地下に広がる20m角四方、高さ15mの土でできた空間を考えた。地下空間の上部は空に向かって開かれていて、空や島の木々といった自然、光や風を感じられ、島に流れる小川が上部から小さな滝となって落ちてくる。

ここでは、お墓や祈りの場などの場所と自然が融合する。人間の生死と自然のダイナミズムの一体化を感じられる場所を目指した。(西沢立衛)

This graveyard concept was planned for a small, uninhabited island in the Seto Inland Sea and the shore across the water. The shore is occupied by a small accommodation for several people. The uninhabited island features a landing pier, a walking path, graves, a rest area, and a prayer space. After approaching the island from the opposite shore in a small boat, visitors experience the entire island environment as they follow the walking path, enjoy the trees, streams, and nature, and visit the graves and prayer site.

The graves stand in the forest in gaps between the trees and mindful of the lay of the land. They are situated in relation to the gullies, slopes, peak, and trees that surround them, no different than how a person would construct a house.

For the prayer space, we conceived of a space 20 meters square, sunk 15 meters into the earth from the island's peak. This underground space is open to the sky, allowing those inside to feel nature above them from the sky and the trees, the light and the wind, while an island stream trickles into the space as a small waterfall.

In this design, the graves and prayer space harmonize with nature. We aimed to create a place where human life and death feel united with nature's dynamism. (Ryue Nishizawa)

2016.2.18
竣工

2016.4.15
完成記念
料理：吉岡幸宣　お菓子：藤田怜美　お土産：今西善也

2016.4.15–9.9
展覧会「須田悦弘｜彫刻　祇園ない藤｜履物　新里明士｜陶芸」

2016.9.16–12.11
展覧会「内藤礼」

2017.10.7
トーク「石川直樹」

2017.10.28
勉強会「工芸建築」
講師：秋岡雄史（アートディレクター）　三浦史朗（構匠）

2017.12.16
勉強会「食と器｜最期の時、最初の日」
講師：生江史伸（料理）今西善也（お菓子）佐藤聡（ガラス）
中川周士（木工）新里明士（陶磁器）嘉戸浩（唐紙）

2017.12.18–12.20
展覧会「食と器｜最期の時、最初の日」
参加作家：佐藤聡　中川周士　新里明士　嘉戸浩

2018.2.9–2.12
展覧会「花が咲いている方へ」
参加作家：西山隼人（植物）藤田怜美

2018.9.8
トーク「徳田邸」
講師：西沢立衛（建築家）鳥居厚志（現場監督）

2018.9.14
トーク「Place for Life, Energy and Spirit」
講師：桑田卓郎（陶磁器）新里明士

2018.9.15
勉強会「集落：養生と六根」
講師：伊藤東凌（建仁寺塔頭両足院副住職）三浦史朗　三浦誠（鍼灸師）
三浦豊（森の案内人）杉山早陽子（お菓子）

2018.9.16–2019.5.30
展覧会「暮らしの場と祈りの場と眠りの場」
参加作家：嘉戸浩　桑田卓郎　佐藤聡　須田悦弘（現代美術）中川周士
新里明士

2018.9.22
トーク「履物考：ない藤の内藤誠治さんと建築の関川くん
──スニーカーの次って？」
講師：内藤誠治（履物）関川圭基（京都大学大学院）

2019.2.9
トーク「石上純也：建築──自作について」

2019.2.23
トーク「感性と技術と空間」
講師：嘉戸浩　佐藤聡　須田悦弘　中川周士　新里明士

2019.11.4
SEI-kitchen　第1回「きんとん／食と建築」
詳細 p.34

2019.11.10
SEI-kitchen　第2回「おでん－アジア／現代アートの思考法・前編：
アーティストはどんなふうに考えるのか？」
詳細 p.34

2019.12.9
SEI-kitchen　第3回「おでん－イタリア／現代アートの思考法・後編：
ウォルター・デ・マリア」
詳細 p.34

2019.12.23
SEI-kitchen　第4回「おぜんざい／
アートを日本から見る・日本の外から見る」
詳細 p.34

2020.6.1
SEI-kitchen　第5回「あしたの畑──味噌スープランチ」
詳細 p.35

2020.7.19
SEI-kitchen　第6回「あしたの畑──オーガニック・ソウルフード」
詳細 p.35

2020.9.8–10.17
展覧会「あしたの畑──考える小屋」
協働作家：嘉戸浩　坂本健　佐藤聡　中川周士　新里明士　西沢立衛
撮影：森川昇

SEI Activity Log 2016–2020

February 18, 2016
Completion Shinto Ceremony

April 15, 2016
Opening Event
Celebration feast prepared by:
Yukinori Yoshioka, Nawaya (meals); Satomi Fujita, kashiya (sweets); Zenya Imanishi, Kagizen (souvenir sweets)

April 15–September 9, 2016
Inauguration exhibition with sculpture by Yoshihiro Suda (artist), traditional kimono shoes by Seiji Naito, Gion Naito, and ceramic works by Akio Niisato (ceramic artist)

September 16–December 11, 2016
Exhibition "Rei Naito"

October 7, 2017
Talk Event with Naoki Ishikawa (alpinist, photographer and essayist)

October 28, 2017
Study Group "Craft Architecture"
Lecturers: Yuji Akimoto (art director), Shiro Miura (*Sukiya* architect)

December 16, 2017
Study Group "Eating and Vessel | Last time and First day"
Lecturers: Zenya Imanishi on beans, Koh Kado, kamisoe, on paper, Shuji Nakagawa on wood, Shinobu Namae, L'Effervescence, on grains, Akio Niisato on soil, Satoshi Sato, PONTE, on glass

December 18–20, 2017
Special Exhibition "Eating and Vessel | Last time and First day"
Participants: Koh Kado, Shuji Nakagawa, Akio Niisato, Satoshi Sato

February 9–12, 2018
Special Exhibition "To the direction where flower smiles"
Creators: plants and flowers by Hayato Nishiyama, Hanaya Mitate, and sweets by Satomi Fujita

September 8, 2018
Talk Event "Empathy: Architecture"
Lecturers: Ryue Nishizawa (architect), Atsushi Torii (constructor)

September 14, 2018
Lecture "Place for Life, Energy and Spirit"
Lecturers: Takuro Kuwata (ceramic artist), Akio Niisato

September 15, 2018
Study Group "Cure and Six Senses"
Lecturers: Toryo Ito (monk), Shiro Miura, Makoto Miura (acupuncturist), Yutaka Miura (forest guide)
Sweets prepared by Sayoko Sugiyama, Okashimaru

September 16, 2018–May 30, 2019
Special Exhibition "Place for Life, Energy and Spirit"
Participants: Koh Kado, Takuro Kuwata, Shuji Nakagawa, Akio Niisato, Satoshi Sato, Yoshihiro Suda

September 22, 2018
Lecture "Shoes Maze: Future Architecture"
Lecturers: Seiji Naito, Yoshiki Sekikawa (architecture graduate student)

February 9, 2019
Talk Event with Junya Ishigami (architect)

February 23, 2019
Lecture "Art, Technique and Environment"
Lecturers: Koh Kado, Shuji Nakagawa, Akio Niisato, Satoshi Sato, Yoshihiro Suda

November 4, 2019
SEI-kitchen #1 "Seasonal Sweets: *Kinton* (mashed sweet potatoes and chestnuts) / Food and Architecture"
details p.34

November 10, 2019
SEI-kitchen #2 "Oden-Asia / How Would Artist Think When They Create Works of Art?"
details p.34

December 9, 2019
SEI-kitchen #3 "Oden-Italian / Walter De Maria"
details p.34

December 23, 2019
SEI-kitchen #4 "*Zenzai* (sweet red beans soup) / Art How It Is Seen from Japan and Outside of Japan"
details p.34

June 1, 2020
SEI-kitchen #5 "TOMORROW FIELD—Miso Soup Lunch"
details p.35

July 19, 2020
SEI-kitchen #6 "TOMORROW FIELD—Organic Alimentation for Tomorrow"
details p.35

September 8–October 17, 2020
Special Exhibition "TOMORROW FIELD—A Thinker's Cabin"
Developing project with: Koh Kado, Shuji Nakagawa, Akio Niisato, Ryue Nishizawa, Ken Sakamoto, Satoshi Sato
Documented by Noboru Morikawa

西沢立衛
1966年生まれ。1990年横浜国立大学大学院修了。妹島和世建築設計事務所を経て1995年妹島和世とSANAA設立。1997年西沢立衛建築設計事務所設立。
現在、横浜国立大学大学院Y-GSA教授。

徳田佳世
1971年生まれ。オレゴン大学芸術学部卒業。2001年より2010年まで美術活動のキュレーターとしてベネッセアートサイト直島の企画に携わる。2014年株式会社WATER AND ART、2016年NPO法人TOMORROW設立。

Ryue Nishizawa
Born in 1966. Completed a master's degree at the Yokohama National University in 1990. Worked at Kazuyo Sejima & Associates before cofounding SANAA with Kazuyo Sejima in 1995. Established Ryue Nishizawa Architects in 1997.
Currently a professor at the Yokohama Graduate School of Architecture (Y-GSA).

Kayo Tokuda
Born in 1971. Received a degree in art history from the University of Oregon in 1994. Worked as a curator at Benesse Art Site Naoshima between 2001 and 2010.
Established WATER AND ART Inc. in 2014 and founded Non-profit Organization TOMORROW in 2016.

Photo Credits
Noboru Morikawa (p.02, pp.31–32, p.35, p.36 bottom)
Ken'ichi Suzuki (pp.05–09, pp.11–15, p.18, p.24, pp.26–27, p.38)
Office of Ryue Nishizawa (p.10, pp.16–17, pp.36–37)
Yoshiko Watanabe (p.04)
Haruhi Okuyama, Yoshiko Watanabe (pp.33–34)

pp.28–29
Walter Niedermayr
Bildraum S511/2019, Copyright by the artist, Galerie Nordenhake Berlin, Stockholm, Ncontemporary Milan, Galerie Widauer Innsbruck.

Translation: Sam Holden (p.03, p.05, p.11, p.17, p.19, p.25, p.27, pp.36–37)

Copy editing: Eugenia Bell (p.31. p.33)

丗｜SEI／徳田邸——京都 生きる喜び

2020年10月2日 初版第1刷
2023年12月22日　　第2刷

著者：西沢立衛 徳田佳世

デザイン：下田理恵

協力：株式会社WATER AND ART NPO法人TOMORROW
印刷・製本：イニュニック
編集・発行：富井雄太郎

発行所：millegraph
　　　　Tel & Fax 03-5848-9183
　　　　info@millegraph.com
　　　　http://www.millegraph.com/

SEI / Tokuda House —— Kyoto Joy of Life

Date of publication:
2 October 2020 / First edition, first impression
22 December 2023 / Second impression

Author: Ryue Nishizawa　Kayo Tokuda

Design: Rie Shimoda

Cooperation: WATER AND ART Inc.
　　　　　　　 Non-profit Organization TOMORROW
Printing and binding: inuuniq Co., Ltd.
Editing and publication: Yutaro Tomii

Publisher: millegraph
　　　　　Tel & Fax +81-(0)3-5848-9183
　　　　　info@millegraph.com
　　　　　http://www.millegraph.com/